Chardin travelled extensively in Iran and was appointed royal mer  According to Chardin, in the late 17th century, Isfahan housed some 162 mosques, 48 theological colleges and 273 bathhouses. Shah Abbas I began construction of the city in 1590, and by the time it was finished Isfahan had become one of the most beautiful cities in the Middle East.

Private collection, courtesy J.M. Waibel

MEDIEVAL IRAN

Massoume Price

Celestial globe from Isfahan, Iran. Incised bronze. *Louvre Museum, 11th – 13th century*

ANAHITA PRODUCTIONS LTD.
Vancouver – Canada

ANAHITA PRODUCTIONS LTD.
Vancouver – Canada

CULTURE OF IRAN YOUTH SERIES

MEDIEVAL IRAN

Research & Text	**Massoume Price**
Project Director	**Sheereen Price**
Editor	**Freydis Jane Welland**
Art Direction	**Maral Honarbin**
Production	**Maral Honarbin**
	Malinda Dodds
	Shahrzad Akhavan
	Babak Manavi
Photography	**Davood Sadeghsa**
	Masoud Harati
	J.M. Waibel

Medieval Iran / author: Massoume Price ; illustrator: Bita Tabrizi.

(Culture of Iran youth series)
ISBN 978-0-9809714-1-5

1. Iran--History--640- --Juvenile literature. 2. Iran--Civilization--Juvenile literature.
I. Tabrizi, Bita, 1987- II. Title. III. Series: Price, Massoume. Culture of Iran youth series.

DS288.P75 2012   j955'.02   C2010-904789-3

Anahita
PRODUCTIONS

Published by C & C Offset Printing Co. Ltd., China
Sponsored by Zohreh Waibel
Marketing by Zohreh Waibel, Vancouver

www.anahitaproductions.com   info@anahitaproductions.com

Contents

Opposite Page: Gold armlet. *National Museum of Iran, 11th century*

This Page: Shah Abbas II built Khaju Bridge in Isfahan in 1650. It has 23 arches, and is 105 meters long and 14 meters wide. The bridge has gates under the archways, which are used to regulate the river's flow.

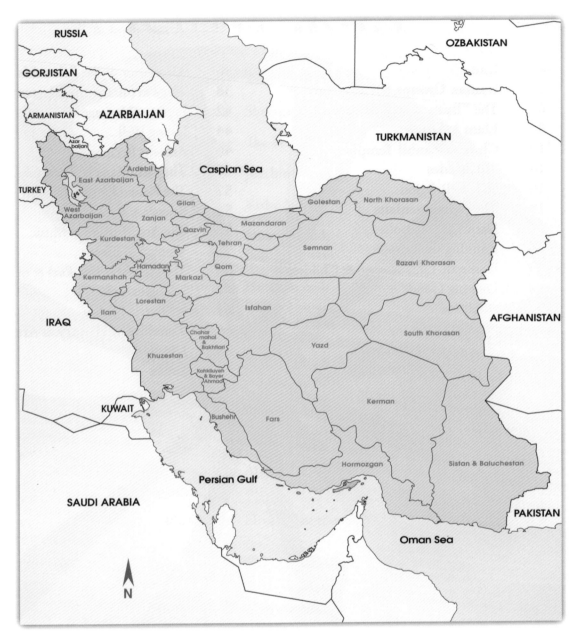

Iran, with a current population of over 70 million people, has a diverse ethnic and religious background. The ancient inhabitants lived as nomads and farmers in a landscape of rugged mountain chains surrounding interior plateaus in the heart of the Middle East. The first agricultural communities in Iran date from 8000 BCE, and by 3000 BCE there were large city-states in southern and eastern Iran, which at times were ruled by the major Mesopotamian powers to the west. About 2700 BCE, Mesopotamian domination was ended for a while by the first local dynasty to rule Iran, the Elamites, whose origin is unknown. The first Iranian groups arrived in Iran in the second millennium BCE from the area around the Aral Sea in Kazakhstan. For a long time the Iranians were subjugated by others, including the Assyrians. In the seventh century BCE the Medes became the first Iranians to rule the area. In 549 BCE another Iranian group, the Persians, overpowered the Medes and founded the Achaemenid Empire, which extended from Egypt to India. Their reign ended when Alexander of Macedonia occupied Iran in 330 BCE. Following his death, his empire was divided and the Greek Seleucid Dynasty of Iran was formed. The Seleucids were defeated in 247 BCE by the next Iranian dynasty, the Parthians—who governed for over 400 years and stopped the Roman armies from expanding east into Iran. In 224 CE, the Sasanian Dynasty emerged, expanded Iranian territories and consolidated Zoroastrianism, which had been the main religion of Iran since the Achaemenid era. This was mostly done to rival Christianity, the state religion of the Roman Empire. The eastern territories of the Roman Empire were known as the Byzantium and included the majority of the Middle East and parts of Africa. Many wars between the Iranians and the Byzantines weakened both and led to the conquest of both empires by the nomadic Arab Muslim forces in the seventh century.

Above: Underground passage and tunnels under Salasel Castle in Shushtar, southern Iran. It was first built during the Achaemenid era and was a major defensive fort during the Sasanian period in the 7th century CE. Such tunnels were part of engineering designs to ventilate and control humidity and to maintain pleasant temperatures during very hot weather. The castle was inhabited until the early 20th century.

The seventh century was a major turning point in the history of the Middle East. Nomads from Arabia conquered Iran and Iraq as well as the Christian Byzantine Empire, which included Egypt, Syria, Jordan, Lebanon, Palestine and Turkey, before expanding further into Africa and Spain. They overpowered the Sasanians, and ruled Iran for over 200 years. They introduced many changes that have transformed Iran culturally and politically ever since. Following the early conquests, Arab military garrisons were established in Iran and this was followed by waves of migrating Arab settlers. They introduced Islam and largely ended Zoroastrianism. The Iranian capital Ctesiphon (outside modern Baghdad) was abandoned and Iraq, which had a large Iranian population was lost. The first powerful Arab dynasty, the Umayyads (661 – 750), promoted Islam and the Arabic language. Iran was divided into mini-states with many different rulers loyal to the Arab caliphs. The acceptance of Islam by the populace was slow. Some of the Iranian ruling groups in the countryside accepted Islam to preserve their power, and helped the local Arab governors. Initially, most Iranians, whether Zoroastrian, Buddhist, Christian or Jewish, maintained their religions and paid taxes for protection. The early converts into Islam were dependent on Arab patronage and did not benefit from privileges the Arabs had, and many revolted. Gradually most Iranians became Muslims to improve their position, gain equality with the Arabs and to avoid the payment of obligatory taxes.

Right: Sasanian royal residence at Cteisphon, known as *Tagh-i-Kasra*, meaning the King's arch. Its design influenced Islamic architecture. The Iranians lost the battles of Qadisiyyah and Nihavand in 637 and 641, which led to the fall of their capital, but kept fighting in major cities. The last king, Yazdgerd III, went to Central Asia and his son Piruz received help from the Tang court in China. After the king was killed in 651 the rest of his family remained in China.

Right: Tari Khaneh in Damghan is the oldest surviving mosque in Iran (9th century). Prophet Mohammad (c. 570 – 632) united various Arabian tribes under the banner of Islam after many battles. Following his death, the conquests expanded out of Arabia. Four of the Prophet's companions, including Ali (his cousin and son-in-law), formed the first Muslim caliphate. Once in Iran, the Muslim rulers promoted building mosques. The pre-Islamic columns suggest that this place was a Zoroastrian temple.

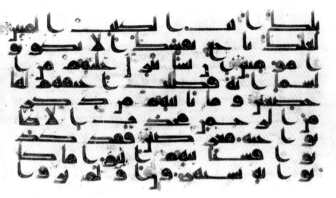

Above: The Qur'an (literally "the recitation") is the sacred text of Islam. The earliest surviving Qur'ans are from the 8th century and were written in the Kufic script. It was nearly two centuries later that the Arabic script developed into its current form. A page from the Qur'an in Kufic script. *Reza Abbasi Museum, Tehran, 8th – 9th century*

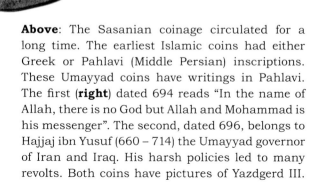

Above: The Sasanian coinage circulated for a long time. The earliest Islamic coins had either Greek or Pahlavi (Middle Persian) inscriptions. These Umayyad coins have writings in Pahlavi. The first (**right**) dated 694 reads "In the name of Allah, there is no God but Allah and Mohammad is his messenger". The second, dated 696, belongs to Hajjaj ibn Yusuf (660 – 714) the Umayyad governor of Iran and Iraq. His harsh policies led to many revolts. Both coins have pictures of Yazdgerd III.

Following the early Islamic conquests, Muslims started fighting amongst themselves and many groups emerged. The Iranians supported Shi'a (meaning "followers") movements against the caliphs. The Shi'ites supported descendants of the prophet from his daughter Fatima and her husband Ali, the fourth caliph, who was assassinated in 661. His death marks the beginning of the division between the Sunni (who recognize all the first four caliphs) and the Shi'ites. In the eighth century, the Iranians sided with relatives of the Prophet Mohammad, the Abbasids (r. 750 – 1258), and overthrew the Umayyad Dynasty in 750. Once in power, the Abbasids let down their Iranian allies and eliminated their leaders. Culturally, the Iranians maintained identity through their language. The pre-Islamic "Middle Persian" Pahlavi script evolved into Arabic script, but the Persian language, which is Indo-European, remained and gradually "New Persian" or "Farsi Dari" emerged. Many of the existing pre-Islamic texts on history, literature and sciences were translated from Pahlavi into Arabic and re-written in New Persian. By the tenth century, New Persian replaced Arabic and became the standard language and script of Iran and the eastern territories of the caliphate.

Left: Early Islamic artistic traditions in Iran remained firmly based on pre-Islamic Sasanian styles. On this gold plated silver plate, the central figures resemble Sasanian motifs and the edges have calligraphy in Arabic Kufic script. *Reza Abbasi Museum, Tehran*

Right: Iran was a major exporter of textiles during the Sasanian period. Textiles remained important in the medieval period. Sasanian designs had a lasting impact throughout the Muslim Empire. They had no Islamic religious symbolism and could be exported to Christian countries that were major trade partners at the time. Textile fragment, silk with Sasanian style roundels. Buyid era. *The National Museum of Iran*, 9th – 10th century

Below: The Falak ol Aflak Castle in Luristan has been continuously inhabited for around 1800 years. Built by the Sasanians in the 3rd century, it was occupied for over two centuries by the Arab rulers of Luristan. By the 10th century it was in the hands of the Iranian Buyid Dynasty that had captured the castle from a local Kurdish ruling group. The castle has a large Anthropology Museum and one of its most significant features are the underground tunnels built by the Sasanian engineers to de-humidify and ventilate the structure.

Gold tray from early Islamic period with Kufic inscriptions around the edges. *Reza Abbasi Museum, Iran*

It took four hundred years for Islam to be established in Iran. The new religion introduced changes in society and at the same time was influenced by many Iranian elements. The interior of early mosques remained close to that of Sasanian royal halls. The Persian innovation of raising domes over a square hall became a characteristic of Islamic architecture. As Islam prescribes veiling for women and separation of men and women in public places, new architectural styles emerged. Inner courtyards and the construction of secluded women's quarters to maintain privacy for women became a feature of Islamic architecture. Theatrical and musical performances, which were part of many Zoroastrian festivals, were not performed at mosques. However, music was played at the caliphs' courts. Historians mention hundreds of Iranian musicians—including chorus girls from Khorasan—singing songs at the Abbasid court in Baghdad about the pre-Islamic Iranian hero Siavash. Mystical sects known as Sufi emerged in the tenth century, revolving around loyalty to individual leaders with strict practices. Also, many elements from Zoroastrianism found new forms of expression in the new religion, particularly in Iranian Shi'ism, which gradually gained support.

Above: This ancient temple in Maragheh has Arabic writings on the right wall. The temple was very likely dedicated to the pre-Islamic Iranian deity Mithra known as Mihr in modern Persian. In the 9th century a small Shi'a sect called Zaydi dominated northern Iran. The ruling Buyids in 936 performed the first public ceremony mourning Ali's son, Imam Hussein, killed by the Umayyad supporters in 680 in Karbala. However, most Iranians remained Sunni up to the 16th century.

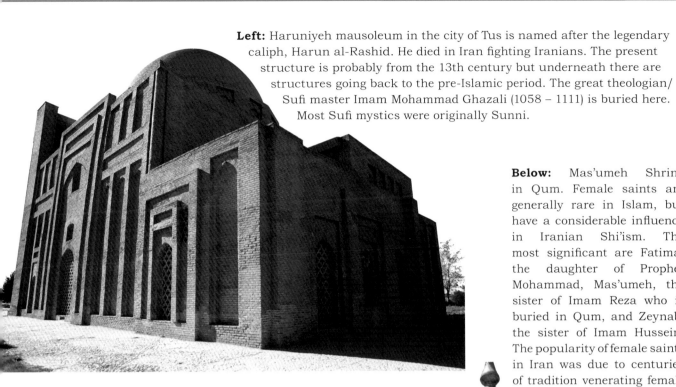

Left: Haruniyeh mausoleum in the city of Tus is named after the legendary caliph, Harun al-Rashid. He died in Iran fighting Iranians. The present structure is probably from the 13th century but underneath there are structures going back to the pre-Islamic period. The great theologian/ Sufi master Imam Mohammad Ghazali (1058 – 1111) is buried here. Most Sufi mystics were originally Sunni.

Below: Mas'umeh Shrine in Qum. Female saints are generally rare in Islam, but have a considerable influence in Iranian Shi'ism. The most significant are Fatima, the daughter of Prophet Mohammad, Mas'umeh, the sister of Imam Reza who is buried in Qum, and Zeynab, the sister of Imam Hussein. The popularity of female saints in Iran was due to centuries of tradition venerating female deities such as Anahita in pre-Islamic Iran.

Bottom Left: Semi precious stones, early Islamic period. The Zoroastrians respected 12 holy beings whose names are the names of the twelve Iranian months in the Persian calendar. They also believed in the appearance of special beings to save the world. The last one, Saoshyant will raise the dead, followed by the last judgment. The Iranian Shi'ites believe in similar concepts, twelve *imams* and the coming of a liberator (Mahdi) at the end of the time and the last judgment.

The early caliphs relied heavily on experts from Iran, Egypt and Syria to run their affairs. The most celebrated Iranians that worked at the Abbasid court included the Barmakid (723 to 803) and the Nawbakhti families (712 to 924) and Fazl bin Sahl Zadan-Farrukh, the chief minister to caliph al-Ma'mun (786 – 833). Iranians in Baghdad wrote in Arabic and were responsible for advancing the arts and sciences, and many are known as the pillars of the Islamic civilization. They supported Iranian scientists, administrators and artists, and fashioned the Abbasid court in the manner of the Sasanians. Arabic grammar was composed in the 8th century and the most famous grammarian was Sibawayh Farsi. His grammar book *Kitab Sibawayh* is one of the earliest books in Arabic and one of the greatest books about linguistics. The most famous director of the Baghdad library was the great Iranian nationalist and Pahlavi expert, Musa Sahl ibn-Harun (d. 830). The famed Iranian mathematician and astronomer Khwarizmi (c. 800 – 847) was employed full time by the library at this time. He introduced the term "algebra" and a distorted version of his name in Latin gives us the word "algorithm". Other celebrated Iranians included: Zakariya Razi (864 – 930) who discovered alcohol and is regarded as the father of modern chemistry, Abu-Nasir Farabi (c. 870 – 950) a major philosopher and scientist who wrote on musical theory, and Abu-Rayhan Biruni (973 – 1048) who was a master physicist, astronomer, meteorologist, historian, geographer and philosopher.

Left: Mohammad Bukhari's (810 – 870) mausoleum in Samarkand, Uzbekistan. Bukhari is the author of the most important collection of Islamic religious literature known as *hadith*. Born into a well-known literary Iranian family, his collection of the Islamic narratives (*hadith*) known as *Sahih Bukhari* is regarded as the most authentic account of the Prophet's life and practices by the Sunni Muslims.

Above:
The astrolabe
is an ancient astro-
nomical device used for solving problems relating to
time and the position of the Sun and stars in the sky.
National Museum of Iran, 14th – 16th century

tomb of Avicenna (Ibn Sina, 980 – 1037) in Hamadan Iran. Avicenna is one of the most celebrated scientists
philosophers of the medieval period. He was a master of medicine, physics, mathematics, logic and philosophy.
book, *Canon of Medicine* (*Qanun*) remained the principal authority in medical schools both in Europe and in
a until the early 18th century. His works were translated into Latin as early as the 12th century. Avicenna's
b was re-built over the ruins of the old tomb by Houshang Seyhoun in 1951.

Above: For over two hundred years Persian, Greek and Syriac speakers translated thousands of books into Arabic and spread the ancient knowledge throughout the Middle East and Europe. Roozbeh Parsi (Ibn-al-Muqafa, d. 756) translated the storybook *Kalila & Dimna* from Pahlavi into Arabic. The tales are originally from India. This picture shows a page from an illustrated Persian copy from the 15th century. Hassan Nawbakht (d. 923) the court astrologer, and his son Abu Sahl and other Iranians, translated Pahlavi and Greek texts into Arabic and New Persian. Learned Christian families of Sasanian Iran, such as the Bukhtishu and Masawayh families, were also great translators of texts into Arabic.

Above: This Sasanian Palace is in Firuzabad, Fars. The city's round design can be seen via aerial photography. The roundness of the city of Baghdad in the Abbasid era is identical to the city of Firuzabad. Baghdad is a Persian word meaning God-given. It was a suburb of Ctesiphon. It was chosen as the site of the new Abbasid capital in 762 by Caliph al-Mansur. The city was designed by master Iranian architects Nawbakht, a former Zoroastrian, and Mashallah, a former Jew from Iran.

Above: The famous library of Baghdad was fashioned after the Sasanian Imperial Library and had the same name "The House of Knowledge". *Kitab-al-Fihrist* by Ibn al-Nadim from Baghdad lists hundreds of books written by Iranians. This page from a later copy of the book *The Benefits of Animals*, by Ibn Bakhtishu explains how human eggs are fertilized. The book was composed in Maragheh in Iran. *The Pierpont Morgan Library, New York, Art Resource , c. 1297 – 1300*

From the 9th century, Iranian groups gradually replaced the Arabs in Iran. The Tahirids (820 – 873), Saffarids (873 – 900), the Samanids (893 – 1005) and Buyid (945 – 1055) were amongst such groups. The Buyid occupied Baghdad and sided with the Shi'ites to diminish the power of the caliphs. Eastern Iranian territories including Samarkand and Bukhara in modern Uzbekistan became centers of the new Iranian dynasties. The Samanids supported the arts, and architecture, promoted Iranian culture and encouraged poets, authors and religious writers to compose their works in Persian. The earliest major surviving literary work in modern Persian is by Rudaki (858 – 941) the court poet to the Samanid ruler Nasr II (r. 914 – 943) in Bukhara. Abu-ali Balami, the historian and grand vizier, began to translate the most important history of Islam—*The History of Tabari* written by the Iranian historian Mohammad Jarir-Tabari—from Arabic into Persian in 963. In the late 10th century, Ferdowsi, the legendary Iranian poet, started composing *Shahnameh*: the tales of the ancient pre-Islamic Zoroastrian mythology and Iranian kings. *Shahnameh* became a symbol of Iranian identity and is still read by Iranians. During this period, Turkic mercenaries and slaves became influential and eventually created the first Turkic dynasty in Iran, the Ghaznavids.

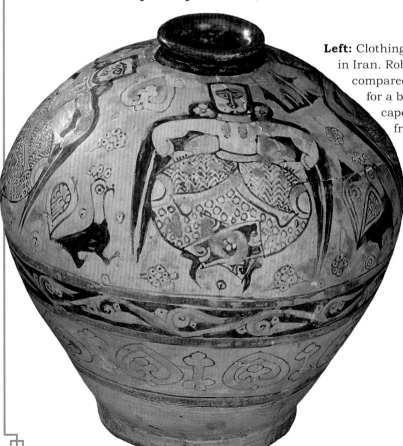

Left: Clothing styles gradually changed in Iran. Robes and coats became longer compared to the Sasanian era and for a brief period pointed shoulder capes were popular, an influence from the orient. Ceramic jar from the city of Nishapur, showing a male dignitary. *Reza Abbasi Museum, Tehran, 10th – 11th century*

Above: Jabaliya Tower. The hexagonal canopy tomb in Kirman in southeastern Iran is dated to the Buyid period in the 11th century and is one of the earliest mausoleums of this type in Iran.

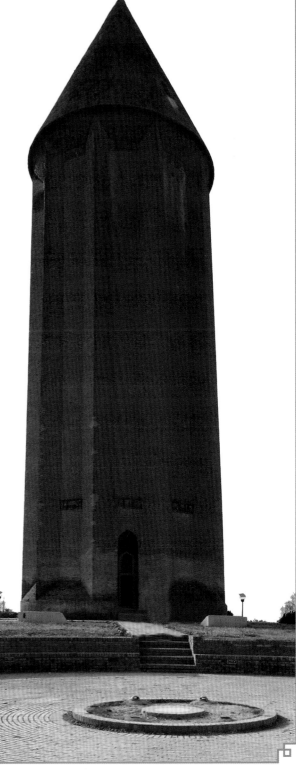

Below: The Zyarids (928 – 1043) ruled over the northern provinces of Iran now known as Gulistan. Qabus Ibn-Voshmgir built this building in 1006 as his tomb. Biruni, the celebrated Iranian scientist worked for this ruler and dedicated one of his works to Qabus. Biruni wrote 146 books and articles mostly in Arabic. *Gunbad-i-Qabus mausoleum*

Left: This tomb in Bukhara belongs to Ismail Samanid (r. 893 – 907) and its architecture represents the transition from Sasanian styles to that of early Islamic architecture in Iran. This is one of the most important examples of early post-Islamic architecture and the structure is so well built, that it has survived for 1100 years without much repair.

Left: The oldest illustrated *Shahnameh* manuscript is from the Mongol period. This page is from a 15th century manuscript. *Reza Abbasi Museum*

Right: Ferdowsi (c. 940–1019 or 1020) was born in modern Khorasan. It took him 30 years to compile his masterpiece *Shahnameh*, the national epic of Iran. The book revived the Persian language following over 300 years of decline. Its stories have been illustrated by artists and have been recited by storytellers in public places for a millennium. *Shahnameh* reading classes are very popular amongst Iranians. Ferdowsi's tomb in Tus and a modern sculpture of Ferdowsi from Tehran.

By the 10th century, many Turkic tribes from Central Asia had already moved into Iran. Their arrival had started in the seventh century when the Iranian Sogdian rulers in eastern Iran asked for their help against the Arab armies. They gradually overthrew the mostly Shi'a Iranian dynasties in Iran and supported Sunni Islam. The Ghaznavids (977 – 1040), Seljuqs (1040 – 1157) and the Khawrazmshahian Dynasty (1157 – 1221) were amongst such groups. The Turkic groups were mostly nomadic and lived in camps. They brought their language, tents, music, food and clothing with them and eventually most settled. They were Turkic speakers, but kept the Persian language and employed the experienced Iranians to run their courts. The Seljuqs were the most influential of all the Turkic groups and ruled over many territories in Central Asia, Iran and Turkey. They defeated the Ghaznavids, occupied Baghdad and declared themselves protectors of the caliphs and at the same time reduced the caliph's powers. During the Seljuqs rule, the Turkic impact was considerable and distinctive art forms with Turkic influence emerged. The Turkic population of modern Iran is mostly from this period. Currently about 28% of Iranians are Turkic speakers. A new Shi'a sect known as the Ismaili, supporters of Ismail, son of Jaffar al-Sadiq the sixth Shi'a *imam*, also gained influence in Iran.

Left: The Turkic rulers of Iran supported Sunni Islam against the expansion of the Shi'a Fatimid rulers of Egypt and the influence of the Ismaili Shi'a missionaries in Iran. The Ismailis have survived. This structure, Ghonbad Kabood in Maragheh is an example of Seljuq architecture and displays intricate brick and tile work.

Colourful tiles with human figures were used to decorate the palaces and homes of the rich. Representations of the planets and zodiac signs, birds, courtiers, musicians and horsemen were popular motives in Seljuq artwork. **Above:** Metal works from the period are superb. Metal box. *Reza Abbasi Museum, Tehran, Seljuq era.*

Above: Bowl. *Seljuq era.* The most celebrated Iranian, Nizam al-Mulk (1018 – 1092) who served two Seljuq kings, also wrote *The Book of Government (Siyasat Nameh)*. He supported Sunni scholarship and expanded and reformed the schools known as *madrassa* that still exist as religious schools. *Reza Abbasi Museum, Tehran, 11th – 12th century*

Omar Khayyam (1044 – 1131) the famous Iranian mathematician and poet, created the current Iranian solar calendar, which was the most accurate one until the 20th century. Khayyam's poems *Rubaiyat* were translated by Edward Fitzgerald in 1859 in England and became such a sensation that Khayyam Clubs were set up. The London Club formed in 1892 is still in existence. Omar Khayyam's tomb in Nishapur was designed by Houshang Seyhoun in 1959.

Above: Seljuq art in Iran is a mixture of Persian, Islamic, and Central Asian-Turkic elements. One of its distinct features is the use of animated script, with the letters transformed into animal and human shapes. Craftsmen from the period mastered metal working techniques with bronze, copper, silver, brass and gold. They also introduced white quartz-based ceramics imitating Chinese porcelain. Tile fragment. *Reza Abbasi Museum, Tehran, 12th century*

Following the arrival of the Arab and Turkic groups, the arts remained Iranian in character but new styles like Arabesque, a mixture of Sasanian and Byzantium art with repeating plant and floral patterns, emerged. While imagery of humans and animals was not used in mosques, shrines and religious schools, it was employed in textiles, books and on wall frescos in the homes of the rich. Gradually, stylized Arabic calligraphic writing became very popular and was used for decorating mosques, buildings and artworks. Such influences can be seen in cut glass, fine ceramics and the metalwork produced in Nishapur from around 900. In architecture, the Seljuqs made grand tombs popular. Textiles, carpets, rugs and expensive fabrics and dress were used to display prestige and wealth. Most people kept wearing clothes made from wool (*pashm*), cotton (*panbeh*) and linen (*katan*). The wealthy also used silks and damasks, and wore gold jewellery decorated with pearls, rubies and emeralds. Music was popular amongst the elite and local musical traditions continued in Iran. From pre-Islamic times the Arabs introduced Iranian elements into their own music. They adopted the 'Persian lute' (*rud*) and made it the principal instrument of the urban and court music. Its Arabic name *ud* is very likely derived from the Persian word *rud*.

Calligraphy is used extensively to decorate mosques. This early example shows writing in Kufic script.
Congressional mosque of Semnan in northern Iran, 10th – 11th century

Right: The art of pre-Islamic Iran had a particularly strong impact on the development of early Islamic metalwork, in which traditional forms and techniques were used. For example, gilded silver, a favorite material for metal works in Sasanian times has remained popular ever since. Plate. *Reza Abbasi Museum, Tehran, 10th century*

Above: Three types of non-figural decorations are used in Islamic art: geometric, vegetal patterns and calligraphy. Geometric patterns are used in architecture and on all kinds of objects. Geometric, vegetal shapes and intricate patterns existed before Islam among the Greeks, Romans, and Iranians. These ancient traditions were used to create new Islamic decorative patterns. Stucco decorations: Nishapur, 10th century post-Islamic (**left**), and Cteisphon (**right**) Sasanian era. *Courtesy Metropolitan Museum of Art, New York*

Right: Musicians. Silver plate in Sasanian style. Iranian musicians greatly influenced the music of the time. In the 9th century, Sarakhsi Khorasani (d. 907 or 908) wrote six books on music. Farabi (870–950) utilized Greek interpretations of music, and in his *Book of Music* mentions the characteristics of Khorasani music and instruments from the region. He was one of the founders of the Baghdad School of Music. In the 9th century, another Iranian, Zaryab founded the Cordoba School of Music in Spain. *British Museum, Art Resource New York, 8th century*

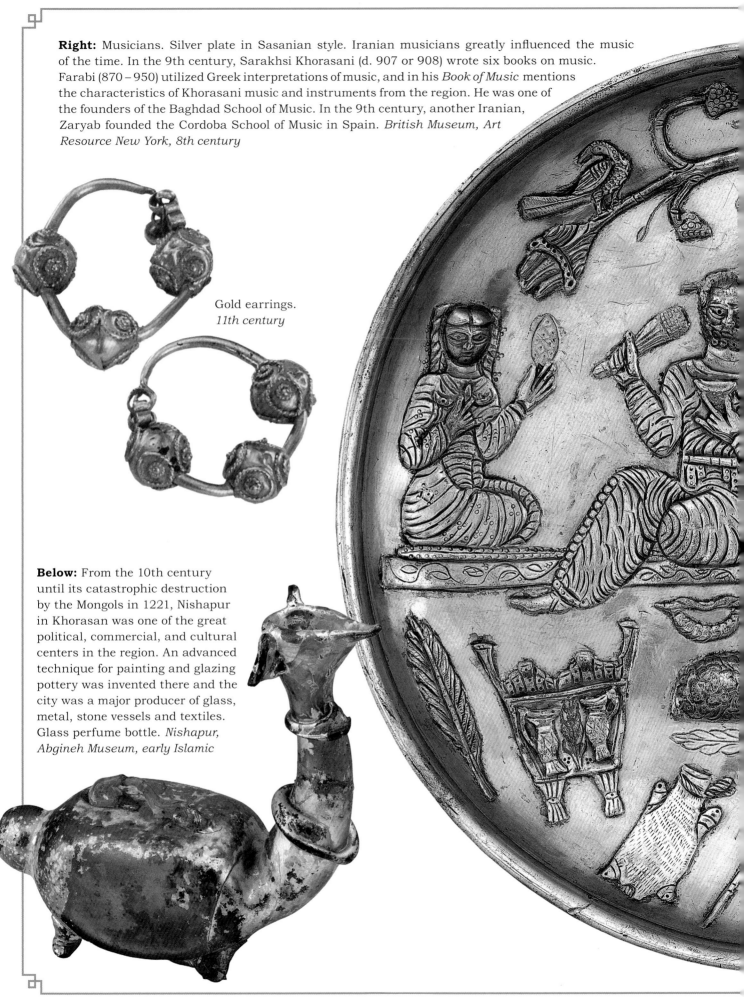

Gold earrings.
11th century

Below: From the 10th century until its catastrophic destruction by the Mongols in 1221, Nishapur in Khorasan was one of the great political, commercial, and cultural centers in the region. An advanced technique for painting and glazing pottery was invented there and the city was a major producer of glass, metal, stone vessels and textiles. Glass perfume bottle. *Nishapur, Abgineh Museum, early Islamic*

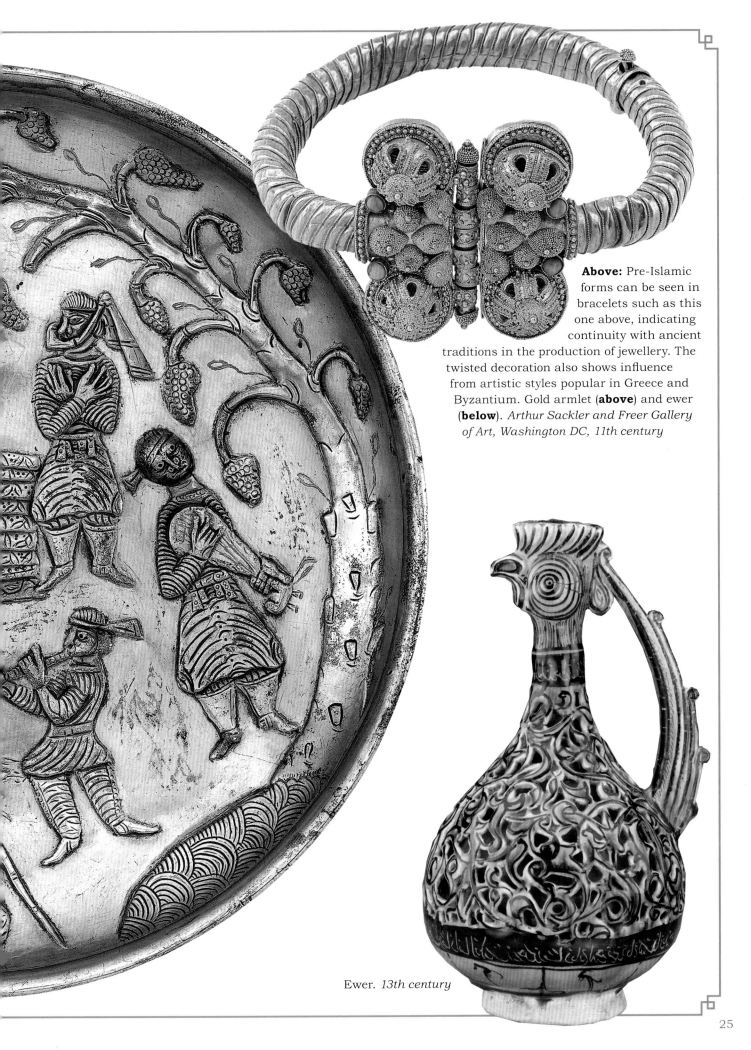

Above: Pre-Islamic forms can be seen in bracelets such as this one above, indicating continuity with ancient traditions in the production of jewellery. The twisted decoration also shows influence from artistic styles popular in Greece and Byzantium. Gold armlet (**above**) and ewer (**below**). *Arthur Sackler and Freer Gallery of Art, Washington DC, 11th century*

Ewer. *13th century*

While early Islamic accounts mention participation of women in the battles and the public affairs of the period, such practices had ceased by the eighth century. Medieval Islamic societies were male-dominated and the religious codes, which regulated many aspects of life, were strictly followed. The development of four schools of Islamic law lead to interpretations of specific verses in the Qur'an and emphasized the importance of male-dominated family units with restrictions on women's activities. The Islamic dress code (*hijab*) and the separation of unrelated men and women had an effect on women's participation in public life. The poor women worked for wealthy ladies as beauty consultants, bath attendants, servants, dressmakers and midwives. Others stayed at home doing crafts and weaving carpets. The law permitted women to keep their parental inheritance and properties, and marriage contracts could protect rich women. Despite the restrictions, several rich and powerful women emerged amongst the ruling classes and some built major charitable foundations and mosques. Others, like the mother of the Samanid ruler, Nuh ibn-Mansur (r. 975 – 997), helped the younger monarchs take the throne and occasionally reigned on their behalf. In the villages and amongst the nomads, most women did not wear veils, had more freedom of movement, and worked with their family members in the fields. Non-Muslim women had more freedom and worked as peddlers going house-to-house, selling different products.

Right: Ceramic showing a couple. The medieval family was extended with close relatives. Men could have four wives by law but most had only one. Rich women spent their days supervising household chores, praying, sewing and making embroidered materials. Marriages were arranged and carried out at an early age. The ceremonies were expensive affairs and lasted for several days. *Reza Abbasi Museum, Tehran, 10th century*

Below: Jar. *Seljuq era.* One of the most influential women of the Turkic dynasties in Iran was Terkan Khatun, the wife of Malikshah Seljuq (1072 – 1092). Another influential woman was Zahideh Khatun who helped her husband in the administration of Fars in central Iran. Her husband, Amir Atabak Bozameh (ca. 1147 – 1168) was buried in the *madrassa* that she built in Shiraz. *Reza Abbasi Museum, Tehran, 12th – 13th century*

Above: Ceramic showing a couple. Amongst the Turkic groups, many high-ranking wives participated in charity and public affairs in addition to court politics. They are abundantly portrayed on ceramics and tiles, and examples of clothing from the period can be seen on such objects. *Reza Abbasi Museum, Seljuq era, 13th century*

Below: Perfume bottle. Cosmetics were a major industry. Kohl was used as eyeliner and hands and feet were painted with henna. White powder and rouge were applied to the face. Beauty spots were popular. Camphor, aloes and sandalwood were used in aromatherapy. Hair and skin products are mentioned in the scientific texts. Refined animal greases were applied as creams and rare and expensive oils were scented with imported fragrant resins and essences. *Abgineh Museum, Tehran, 11th – 12th century*

Kohl

Henna

Genghis Khan (ca. 1162 – 1227) from Central Asia, in 1221 attacked Iran. By 1258 his grandson Hulagau (r. 1256 – 1265) had subjugated most of Iran and ended the Abbasid Caliphate in Baghdad. Several major cities in Iran were destroyed and thousands of people vanished. Large numbers of Mongolian and Turkmen tribes migrated to Iran. Many farms became grazing lands, and food production was reduced. Thousands of Iranians migrated to other countries including the Iranian mystic and poet, Jalal al-Din Rumi whose father had moved with his family from Balkh (Afghanistan) to Konya in modern Turkey. The Mongols ruled over Iran, Azerbaijan, Georgia, Armenia and Iraq for more than one hundred years. In Iran, they formed the Ilkhanid Dynasty. Ilkhan means lesser chief, and implied they were subjects of the greater Mongol Khan in China. They converted to Islam, adopted and spread the Persian language, and partially rebuilt the country. Tabriz in Azerbaijan became the capital and a thriving city. Travelling became easier and the legendary Silk Road went through many Iranian cities. The famous Venetian traveler Marco Polo (1254 – 1324) visited Iran on his way to China. Oriental trends influenced arts, crafts and clothing. Luxury textiles produced in Iran at this period were popular from China to Europe and new musical instruments were imported from the Orient.

This tomb in Shiraz belongs to the master Iranian poet and prose writer Sa'di (ca. 1200 – 1291). He was educated in the famous Nizamieh School of Baghdad (built by Nizam al-Mulk). His two major works *The Orchard (Bustan)* and *The Rose Garden (Gulistan)* were taught and memorized by Iranians for centuries. Goethe and Emerson both admired Sa'di.

A few lines of Sa'di's poetry adorn the Hall of Nations in the United Nations building in New York:

Of one essence is the human race
Thusly has creation put the base
One limb impacted is sufficient
For all others to feel the mace
The unconcerned with others' plight
Are but brutes with human face

Sa'di Shirazi

Illustrated page from the book *Universal History* by the Iranian minister Rashid al-Din (1247 – 1318). The Mongols united Chinese, Islamic, Iranian and Central Asian nomadic cultures and expanded trade and arts. This work from Tabriz shows an oriental influence and portrays a khan and his wife at court in Tabriz. *Staatsbibliothek zu Berlin, Stiftung Preussischer Kulturbesitz, Berlin, Germany, Art Resource, ca. 1330*

The Mongols encouraged the production of illustrated manuscripts. New ideas and Chinese motifs were introduced. Popular subjects included stories from books such as *Shahnameh*. This page is from a later version of "Universal History" by Rashid a-Din and is influenced by Iranian styles. *Reza Abbasi Museum, 14th century*

The tomb of Uljaytu (r. 1304 - 1316) in Sultaniya in northwest Iran is the best surviving example of architecture from the Ilkhanid period. Characteristic features include massive size, extensive use of brick and colourful glazed tiles, and a unique arch that was developed to cover large open areas without the use of columns. This building is the largest brick structure of its kind in the world, and is a world heritage site.

The end of the Ilkhanid Dynasty in 1335 resulted in a power vacuum in Iran, with three short-lived dynasties: the Jalayirids, Muzaffarids and Sarbadaran, and many wars amongst various power groups. At the end of the fourteenth century Tamerlane (lame Timur, r. 1370 – 1405) from Uzbekistan successfully invaded Iran. Timur's campaigns and subsequent forced migrations changed the ethnic mix in Iran and led to decades of civil war between different factions after his death. The Uzbeks gradually lost control over many of their territories in Iran. During his campaigns Timur supported artists and spared their lives. He took many skilled people from Iran back with him to transform his capital, Samarkand, in modern Uzbekistan, into one of the most beautiful cities of the time. Persian remained the language at his court. His support of the arts and Persian literature spread the Iranian influence further in Central Asia. The city of Herat (now in Afghanistan) was Timur's first major conquest in Iran and became another important cultural centre. The illustrated manuscripts known as The Herat School of Persian Miniatures were produced in this city. The Timurids supported Sufi mystical sects and built many mausoleums and shrines to honour Sufi leaders. The Timurid period also witnessed the emergence of women as active patrons of architecture and charitable foundations.

Left: Samarkand was founded in the 7th century BCE. It was originally known as Afrasiab. The city was destroyed by the Mongols, and rebuilt by Timur. The monumental architecture that has survived closely resembles that of Iranian cities. This picture from the Timurid Samarkand shows the similarity of the architectural styles with Iranian cities. The Timurid Empire made the eastern Iranian territories into centers of culture and art.

Above: Hafiz Shirazi (1315 – 1390) created the most popular poetry book in Iran, *The Collected Works of Hafiz* (*Divan Hafiz*). The tomb of Hafiz in Shiraz has become a pilgrim site visited every year by thousands.

Left: Timurid ruler and astronomer Ulugh Beg (1394 – 1449) built this huge observatory in Samarkand with three large astronomical instruments and a solar clock. There was a gigantic arc running through the building's center with its upper end at the rooftop at a height of 40 meters. The Iranian astronomer Mohammad Hussein Birjandi describes the observatory in his astronomical tract *Sharh al-Tadhkira* written in 1507.

Above: In 1404 the ambassador to Henry III of Castile, Ruy González de Clavijo visited Iran. He describes the city of Tabriz as a rich city with well-ordered streets kept secure by guards. He mentions mosques with blue and gold tiles, fine baths, fountains, large buildings, and many bazaars. This page from *Shahnameh* shows a grand house decorated with tiles, a pavilion and a garden. *Gulistan Palace Museum, 1430*

Below: The Herat, Tabriz and Shiraz Schools of miniatures were popular. The Jalayirid School from mid-14th century introduced a new feature. Numerous figures are shown one above the other giving the effect of one appearing to be behind the other. This detail from a page from Bayasanghor's (Timur's grandson) *Shahnameh* shows the king, Kay-Khusrau in a battle. *Gulistan Palace Museum, 1430*

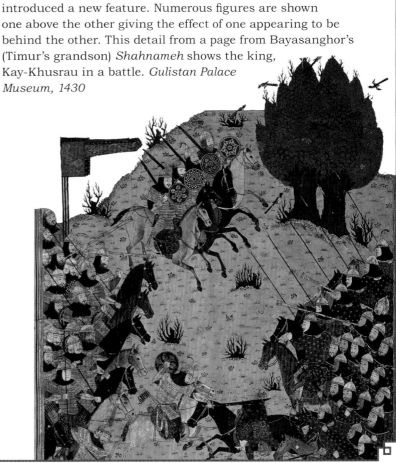

The Turkmen tribes had been invading Iran constantly for decades before and after the collapse of the Timurid rulers. This continued until 1501, when a young Iranian-Turkic nobleman and spiritual leader, Ismail (r. 1501 – 1524) established the Safavid rule in Iran. The Safavids united Iran, created a strong country, built new cities, expanded trade with the Europeans, and supported arts and crafts. Shah Abbas I (r. 1587 – 1629), the most able of the Safavids, strengthened the military and administration, and organized the economy, making Iran a powerful rival to the Ottomans of Turkey. Shah Abbas transformed the ancient city of Isfahan into a new and stunning cosmopolitan commercial center with shops, palaces, mosques, religious schools, a grand bazaar and a huge square in the middle of the city. Isfahan's great square, which still exists, extends more than twenty acres and was the site of polo matches, archery and horse riding contests, ram and bull fighting, wolf baiting and military parades. At night, it was lit by thousands of oil lamps. The inhabitants of Isfahan included Muslims, various European agents and traders, Georgian, Circassian, and Armenian groups and Indians, Muslims and Hindus.

Below: Shah Abbas I built The Image of the World Square (*Naghsh-i-Jahan*) in Isfahan. This picture shows the square as it is now.

Above: Shah Abbas I (r. 1587 – 1629) secured the borders of Iran. He moved his capital from Qazvin to Isfahan in the 1590s and supported Iranian administrators and courtiers. He elevated the ranks of the Armenians, Georgians and Circassians from Caucasus to diminish the power of the Turkmen militants. Shah Abbas and the ruler of Turkistan Vali Nadir Mohammad Khan. *Chihil Sutun Palace, Isfahan*

Historically the kings relied on different armed tribal groups to provide them with fighting forces during the wars. Shah Abbas modernized his army and invited two Englishmen, the Shirley brothers to advise him. *Sword from the Safavid period*

Left: The Safavids partially transformed a tribal nomadic society into a sedentary one and improved agriculture and trade. They combined kingship with religious legitimacy that, with modifications, survived until the 20th century. Chihil Sutun Palace: Shah Tahmasb receiving Humayun, the ruler of India, who came seeking help. *16th century*

Mosque lamp made of silver.
National Museum of Iran, 1614

Sheikh Safi (1252 – 1334), the ancestor of Ismail, started a mystical sect in Ardabil in northwestern Iran, where he is buried. His mausoleum had a library containing a large and priceless collection of manuscripts and miniatures. The collection was handed over to the Russians as part of a treaty in 1828, following a disastrous war. The collection is currently at the Hermitage Museum in St. Petersburg. **Below**: Sheikh Safi's Tomb in Ardabil was rebuilt in the 16th century. **Right**: Helmet. *Freer Gallery of Art & Arthur Sackler Gallery, photo. courtesy A. Soudavar*

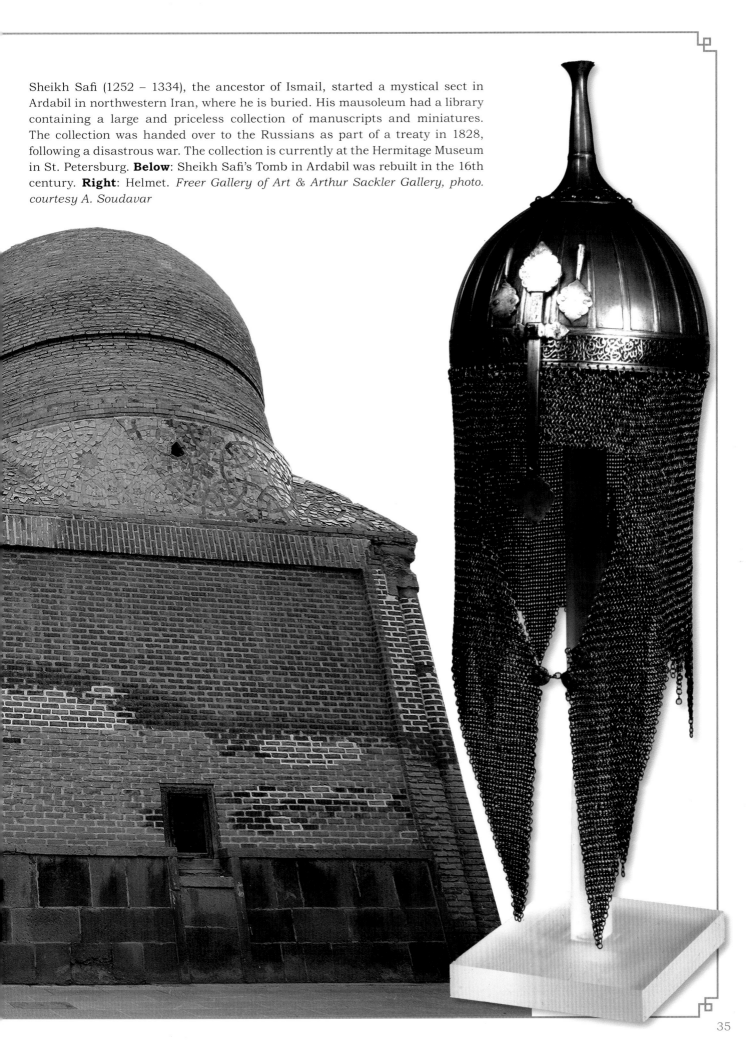

Before Shah Ismail, who made Shi'ism the state religion, most Iranians were Sunni Muslims. His ancestor Sheikh Safi had belonged to a Sufi order with Sunni sympathies. The Sufi, like most mystical groups, try to understand God through their own experiences by practicing meditation, fasting and other similar acts. The Shi'a influence had started with the capture of Shi'a Ottoman soldiers from Anatolia in Turkey in 1429. Over time, the captive soldiers influenced the religion of the Turkmen tribal groups in Iran. Once Shi'ism was declared the state religion, it took over one hundred years and some force to achieve widespread conversion. Many religious schools were created to train clergymen and encourage the adoption of the new religious order in the country. Soon after, an extensive new Shi'a literature emerged that is still in use. This literature created its own distinctive type of Shi'ism by reinforcing themes considered appropriate. Religious compositions included prayer, histories, songs, rituals and ceremonies for mourning the deaths of saints such as Imam Hussein and Imam Ali. Female saints were also elevated and a vast literature about their lives emerged.

Above: Tile. *Safavid Era*

Left: Some artists left Iran for the neighbouring countries to avoid the strict religious codes imposed at times, and others left to experience different artistic cultures. This page is from a collection of paintings known as "Moragha Golshan" created by Iranian artists for the ruler of India. This photo is a close up of a banquet. *Gulistan Palace Museum, 17th century*

Above: By the 17th century most Sunni groups were concentrated around the border areas, as they still are today — in Kurdistan bordering Iraq, eastern Iran in Sistan and Baluchistan bordering Pakistan and Afghanistan, and in Turkmen areas close to Turkmenistan. This picture shows soldiers from Shah Ismail's army. Fresco. *Chihil Sutun Palace*

Descendents of Lebanese immigrants, Mohammed Taqi (1594 – 1659), and his son Baqir Majlesi were pioneer clergymen who created and promoted Iranian Shi'ite literature in the Safavid era. Painting of Baqir Majlisi. *Freer Gallery of Art & Arthur M Sackler Gallery*

Above: Imam Reza Shrine in Mashhad was a Sasanian retreat converted into an Umayyad palace. The Abbasid caliph Harun al-Rashid was buried there. The later burial of Imam Reza, the 8th Shi'a *imam* (9th century) overshadowed Harun's tomb and his remains were moved. The shrine has a 600-year-old library with around 70,000 rare manuscripts and some 6 million historical documents. *Freer Gallery of Art & Arthur Sackler Gallery, photo courtesy A. Soudavar*

Below: Shah Ismail (r. 1501 – 1524) was supported by Turkmen known as the *Qizilbash* "redheads" and was regarded as a saint. His reputation was damaged when large territories — including the major cities of Balkh and Qandahar (now in Afghanistan) were lost to the Ottomans in 1514. This fresco from Chihil Sutun Palace in Isfahan shows Shah Ismail I (**right**) fighting the Uzbek leader Mohammad Shaybani in 1510. His horse is decorated with henna. *Safavid Era.*

Left: The Safavids organized major events such as the mourning rituals for Imam Hussein in the early 1500s. Large groups of men carried symbolic objects and standards (*alam*), some of which were borrowed from other nations. They walked in groups chanting religious verses and praising the fallen saints, as they still do today. This picture shows a standard used during the time of mourning for Imam Hussein. *Safavid era*

Below: Before the Safavids, there were very few Shi'a clergymen in Iran. The early Safavids encouraged large-scale emigration of theologians from southern Lebanon, Bahrain and Syria. These clergymen made Iran the foremost center for Shi'a learning. This picture shows the Shah's Mosque in Isfahan named after Shah Abbas. It is now known as Imam's Mosque. The theological students paid a fee and lived and studied in the side rooms around the courtyards.

In the Safavid era trade with Europe and Asia expanded. The Safavids revived the textile industry by employing a large number of Armenian traders who were relocated to Isfahan by Shah Abbas I. The first printing press was brought to Iran by the Armenians at this time to print materials for their own use. The current Armenian population of Iran is mostly descended from these migrants. The arts were supported and reformed as well. In royal workshops Safavid artists created a new style of miniature painting. Their architects built technically advanced structures like the "Shaking Minarets of Isfahan" which were added to an old fourteenth century mosque. The minarets still exist and they move and shake once a lever is pulled. The Safavid courts were graced with musicians and dancers from Iran, Georgia and Armenia. They wore beautiful colourful clothes made of silk with gold and silver threads and elaborate large turbans with slippers, shoes, boots and clogs made of leather. Contact with non-Muslims was expanded and Christian missionary activities in Iran increased. Iranian merchants and politicians started visiting Europe and high-ranking Europeans visited Iran regularly. Some of these visitors wrote extensively on Iran and many of their books have survived. There was also an artistic exchange between Iran, India and Turkey as well as some influence from the Europeans.

Shah Tahmasb (r. 1524 – 1576) was a master painter and an active patron of arts. Artists from the Turkmen and Timurid court studios worked together and created a new Safavid style of painting. The same designs were applied to textiles and carpets for furnishing the wealthy homes. The Isfahan and Tabriz Schools of paintings are from this period. Safavid miniature and a close-up of Shah Tahmasb. *Chihil Sutun Palace*

Right: Tapestry. European travelers describe large silk-weaving factories in many cities. Velvets became fashionable from this time and both silk and velvet were sought after by the Europeans and the Asian traders. Carpet production was transformed from local crafts into a major commodity for export. The most popular carpets had garden designs with colourful vegetal motifs. *Private collection, 18th century*

Textile. *National Museum of Iran, 17th century*

The Safavid potters continued the earlier traditions and at the same time improved techniques and introduced new styles. One popular form used by the potters was known as *Kubachi*. These are mostly large plates or dishes with a thick white body and glaze decorated with figures of humans, flowers and other similar motifs. *Reza Abbasi Museum*

Left: The German traveler, Adam Olearius, who visited Iran in the 17th century, mentions animal trainers and storytellers, and puppeteers as street entertainment. The main character in the puppet shows was "the bald hero" (*pahlavan kachal*) or a cowardly figure called "the cotton-wool hero" (*pahlavan panbeh*) with an unfaithful wife. The import of coffee, a new commodity, led to the establishment of coffeehouses (*khahvehkhaneh*). Fresco showing entertainers at the court of Shah Abbas II. *Chihil Sutun Palace*

The Shaking Minarets (**above**), and See-o-seh-pol Bridge (**below**) in Isfahan. Shah Abbas I was served by Sheikh Bahai (1546 – 1624), a noted theologian, architect, astronomer, physician, philosopher and mathematician. One of his legacies is a bathhouse famous for its tiny heating system. It still puzzles people: no one knows exactly how it worked. *16th century*

By the sixteenth century many ethnic groups lived in Iran. Iranian groups included the Persians, Kurds, Lurs, Zands, Baluchi, Bakhtiari, and Afghans as well as most peoples in the Caspian Sea areas. The Arabs were mainly in the south. The major Turkic groups included the Afshars, Qajars, and Qashqa'i, Turkmen tribes and many Turkic groups in Azerbaijan. Religious minorities included Sunni Muslims and small groups of Zoroastrians, Christian Assyrians and Armenians and Jews. There was also a large population of Hindus from India who mostly worked for the Iranians and also the Europeans who lived in Iran. Sometimes, the Safavids mistreated the minorities, but on the whole were tolerant. Life was restricted and difficult for most women in medieval times. The affluent urban women remained at home. Many poor and lower class women worked for the rich, or in crafts and textile and carpet production. Concubines existed amongst the Shi'ites, and the Safavid kings and rich men had large harems with many Caucasian women such as the Georgians and Circassians from the neighbouring countries. Some were bought as slaves or captured during wars or received as gifts. In the royal harems some of the women became very influential and were involved in harem intrigues against the kings and royal princes.

Safavid paintings provide us with details of every day life. In the palace scenes, women attendants mostly wear white scarves and work with men in two separate spaces emphasizing the separate worlds in which the men and women lived. Miniature **(left)** showing a bride being taken to her future husband, and tile **(above).** *Reza Abbasi Museum, Safavid era*

Pari Khan Khanum, daughter of Shah Tahmasb, was the most powerful woman at the Safavid court. She was her father's most trusted advisor, and after his death in 1576 was instrumental in helping her brother Ismail II (r. 1576 – 1578) gain the throne against the legitimate heir Sultan Mohammad Khodabandeh. Fresco. *Chihil Sutun Palace*

In 1604 Shah Abbas I relocated 13,000 Armenian families from Armenia to the silk-growing regions of northern Iran. Most perished during the move. Another group was moved to Isfahan and was settled in the Julfa district – which still exists. By the 1630s, this group of Armenians gained prominence in foreign trade in Iran. They created a prosperous neighbourhood with churches, shops and residential and public buildings. Armenian Church in the Julfa district in Isfahan. *17th century*

The creation of the Persian Gulf port, Bandar Abbas, built by Shah Abbas I in 1622, encouraged the British and the Dutch East India companies to expand trade through the Persian Gulf. Many European traders and officials visited and lived in Iran, and many commodities such as textiles were exported to Europe. Frescos. Figures in European clothing. *Chihil Sutun Palace*

The Chronicle of Arakel covers the history of Armenians in Isfahan from 1602, and the Safavid and Ottoman wars in Armenia and Mesopotamia. Arakel Tavrizhetzi (1590 – 1670) was born in Tabriz and worked in a church. The Iranian Jewish writer Babai ibn-Lutf (1617 – 1662), and his grandson Babai ibn-Farhad, wrote about the Jews in Safavid Iran. **Top**: The inside of the Black Church (Qareh Kelisa) built between the 4th and 6th centuries in Azerbaijan. The church is one of the oldest surviving churches in the Middle East. Textile fragments showing Biblical scenes. *National Museum of Iran, 16th century.*

The Afghan Revolt & Nadir Shah Afshar 1722 – 1796

By the eighteenth century, the power of the Safavids was diminishing and there were constant attacks on Iran by the Baluchi groups in Kirman, Afghan tribes in Khorasan, and Arabs and the Uzbeks in the south and northeast. The Safavid policies on Shi'ism, amongst other reasons, led to the revolt and separation of the eastern Iranian territories that are now part of Afghanistan. The people of Afghanistan were Sunni Muslims and many refused to convert when Shah Sultan Hussein tried to force them. They eventually attacked Iran and ended the Safavid rule in 1722. The Afghans were finally stopped and forced out of Iran in 1729 by an officer from the Turkic Afshari tribe named Nadir (r. 1736 – 1796). In 1736, Nadir, who was the regent for a very young Safavid king declared himself the new monarch. He was a brilliant soldier but used excessive violence to enforce his authority. In less than two decades he built an empire extending to Central Asia. Nadir also invaded India and brought back the magnificent jewels that are now the main part of the Crown Jewels of Iran. He also recovered treasures and territories Iran had lost in previous wars. The economic and cultural life of Iran declined during his reign and he died at the hands of his guards in 1747.

Nadir Shah defeated the Mongol ruler of Delhi in 1739. This painting at Chihil Sutun Palace shows the Battle of Carnal that led to the sack of Delhi and shows both Nadir and the Indian ruler, Mohammad Shah.

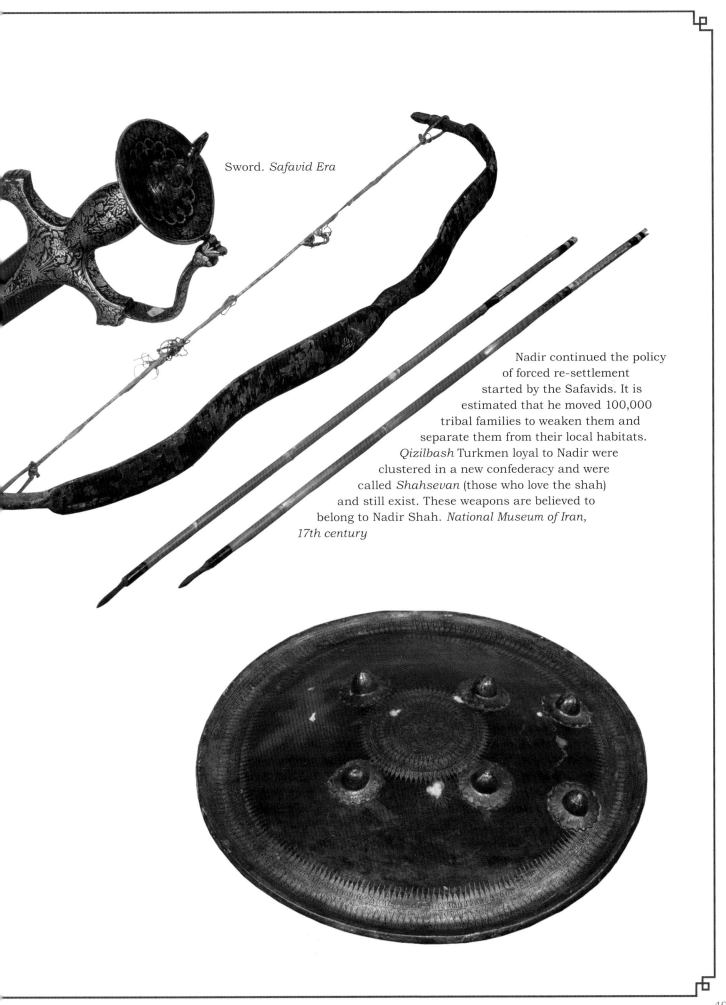

Sword. *Safavid Era*

Nadir continued the policy of forced re-settlement started by the Safavids. It is estimated that he moved 100,000 tribal families to weaken them and separate them from their local habitats. *Qizilbash* Turkmen loyal to Nadir were clustered in a new confederacy and were called *Shahsevan* (those who love the shah) and still exist. These weapons are believed to belong to Nadir Shah. *National Museum of Iran, 17th century*

Nadir in battle. The adoption of Shi'ism isolated Iran at the time. Nadir proposed to the Ottomans that Iranian Shi'ism be accepted as a fifth Sunni sect, to be called *Ja'fari*, after the sixth Shi'a *imam*. Nadir did not succeed in this proposal, and in the process many Shi'ite clergy, fearing for their lives, migrated to Iraq and created an Iranian Shi'ite stronghold near the holy shrines in Karbala and Najaf that still exist. *Gulistan Palace Museum, 18th century*

The Peacock Throne originally
belonged to the Mongol ruler
of India, Shah Jahan, who
built the Taj Mahal. It was
brought to Iran by Nadir
Shah. It was destroyed
following wars in the 18th
century. The throne pictured
here was made in the 18th
century for the coronation of
Fath Ali Shah Qajar, based
on written descriptions of
the Peacock Throne. Carpet.
*National Museum of Iran,
Safavid era*. Peacock Throne
and Jewellery. *The Crown
Jewels Collection of Iran*

Iran went through another period of disorder after Nadir's death. The country became more stable when Karim Khan (r. 1750 – 1779) from the Zand tribe defeated all competitors. By 1760, he controlled all of Iran except Khorasan. He made the country secure and ended forty years of wars. He chose to call himself regent (*vakil*) rather than king. He made the ancient city Shiraz in central Iran the capital. The current bazaar and the finely designed public bath, *Hamam Vakil*, now a museum in Shiraz, were both built by Karim Khan. He reformed the taxation system and supported and attracted many scholars, artists and poets to his capital. The influence of the European artistic styles is seen in the paintings and frescos from the period. By 1722 the Russians under Peter the Great fully established control over all Iranian territories north of the Aras River with the exception of the area that is now the Republic of Azerbaijan. In 1789 Lotf Ali Khan (r. 1789 – 1794), the last Zand monarch, tried to put down a rebellion led by the ruler of the Qajar Turkic group and was defeated. He was a popular figure and his defeat and betrayal at the Bam Citadel in Kirman in southeastern Iran entered local folklore. The end of the Zand period in the eighteenth century marks the beginning of the modern era in Iran.

The Zands were a pastoral tribal Shi'ite group from the Zagros Mountains. They were considered as Lurs and Kurds by historians in the 18th century, and currently are regarded as Lurs. Fortifications, palaces, mosques and other civil and public amenities were built in Shiraz and some have survived. This citadel in Shiraz was built by Karim Khan and is named after him. *Arg-i-Karim Khani*

Above: Karim Khan's royal image was more relaxed. Instead of formal royal portraits, Karim Khan is shown doing ordinary things such as smoking a water pipe. His reign marked the start of court artist Mirza Baba's career, which continued in the following Qajar era. This fresco, from the Zand period is in the Pars Museum, which was originally a palace in Shiraz.

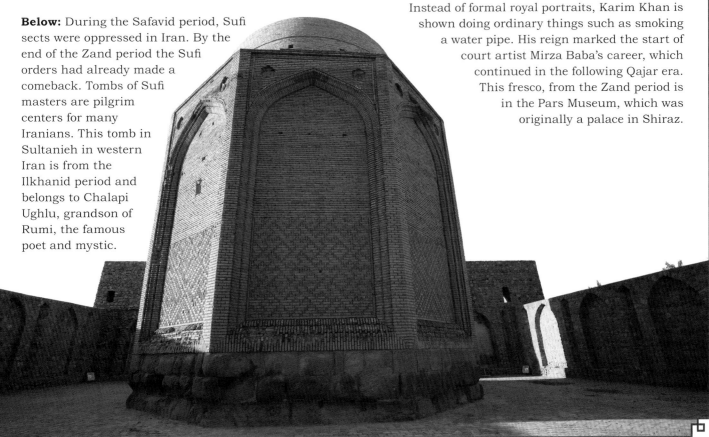

Below: During the Safavid period, Sufi sects were oppressed in Iran. By the end of the Zand period the Sufi orders had already made a comeback. Tombs of Sufi masters are pilgrim centers for many Iranians. This tomb in Sultanieh in western Iran is from the Ilkhanid period and belongs to Chalapi Ughlu, grandson of Rumi, the famous poet and mystic.

Most medieval cities and towns in Iran had a central area that included the main mosque, public baths and the bazaar with separate quarters for the different trades and residences close by. Narrow streets served the ordinary one-story houses, usually built around open courtyards. The homes were designed according to the climate and specific features like wind towers were used in hot and dry areas as air-conditioning. Most houses had basements, which were used in very hot weather since they were cool. Shortage of water has always been a major concern in Iran. Since ancient times, Iranians have utilized various technologies and structures to maximize water use and storage. The most ancient system used in Iran *qanat* (underground water aqueducts), consisted of hundreds of shallow wells interconnected underground with channels to direct water from the mountains using gravity. The system has been in use for 3000 years and in the mid 20th century there were still 22,000 *qanats* covering

170,000 miles of underground channels. Every town had one or several water storage reservoirs (*ab anbar*) and rich people had their own share of the *qanat* system as well as private water reservoirs and baths at home. Textiles, cushions and carpets covered the inside of the homes. Residences built for rich people had gardens with pools, an irrigation system, outdoor pavilions and separate quarters for women and children and the servants. The large cities were walled and the gates were closed soon after sunset. Guards checked the streets at night for safety. The best-preserved medieval cities in Iran currently are parts of Isfahan, Yazd and Kirman.

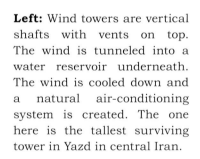

Left: Wind towers are vertical shafts with vents on top. The wind is tunneled into a water reservoir underneath. The wind is cooled down and a natural air-conditioning system is created. The one here is the tallest surviving tower in Yazd in central Iran.

The homes of the wealthy were decorated with luxurious carpets and textiles. The walls often had painted frescos showing people, animals and nature scenes. In this miniature **(above)** a domestic scene is portrayed. *Reza Abbasi Museum, Safavid era*

The earliest reference to polo is from about 600 BCE. The Mongols took the game from Iran to India and the British introduced it in Europe. Miniature. *Arthur M. Sackler and Freer Gallery of Art, photo courtesy A. Soudavar, Safavid era*

Kabood Mosque.
Tabriz, 16th century

Below: Since ancient times, Iranians have had great respect for poets and poetry. Farid al-Din Attar (1145 – 1221) was a chemist, pharmacist and mystic poet from Nishapur who died during the Mongol invasion. His Sufi masterpiece, *Conference of the Birds,* was made into plays, and became a best-seller in North America. *Attar's mausoleum, Nishapur*

Rich people had private bathhouses with cold
and hot water pools. Most people used
washing bowls such as this one with
an ewer for every day cleaning
of their faces and hands,
particularly before and after
meals. *National Museum
of Iran, 17th century*

Left: Both water and windmills were used in Iran. In the Sasanian times in the 6th century Dezfol, in southern Iran, contained a large collection of water mills that were built alongside the river Dez. This windmill in Yazd shows the inner mechanism used for grinding. The grains were put in the container above, and the round stones below energized by the wind, rotated and crushed the grains.

Below: This fort in Rayen in Kirman shows the structure of small medieval towns along the main highways. The ruler and important essential personnel lived inside the fort while others were outside the walls. The towns were walled to protect the inhabitants from invasions. Most agricultural lands were outside the city with water and food storage chambers inside for convenience and in case of a siege.

Above: Cities had various amenities. The building in this picture, now part of a museum in Zanjan in northwest Iran, shows the city's center for laundry and washing clothes. It has a water system and a well-engineered mechanism that circulated and recycled the water to make sure that there was always clean water available.

This alley in Yazd is typical of medieval cities in Iran. The houses had high walls to keep them cool. The walls are re-enforced by the upper bridges. The entire structure is made of mud mixed with straw and other compounds that made them very strong. The streets normally corresponded to a network of water channels that supplied the homes and adjacent fields. **Top (next page)**: The tomb of a mystic in Shahrood, northern Iran.

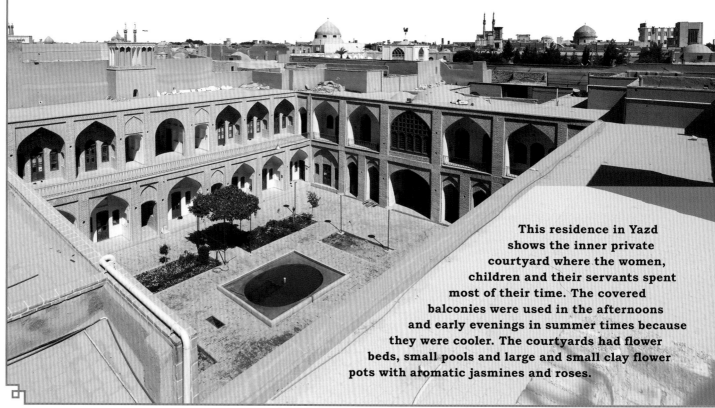

This residence in Yazd shows the inner private courtyard where the women, children and their servants spent most of their time. The covered balconies were used in the afternoons and early evenings in summer times because they were cooler. The courtyards had flower beds, small pools and large and small clay flower pots with aromatic jasmines and roses.

Below: Ice rooms have been built in Iran for centuries and were common in hot climates. They consisted of an inner reservoir, shallow pools and tall walls up to 10 meters high that created shadows over the reservoir to keep it cool. In winter times the water inside the pools froze and ice was formed; the tall walls kept it cool so that the ice could be used in the summer. Ice room in Meybod in central Iran.

Left: This page is from the "Moragha Golshan collection" currently in the Gulistan Palace in Tehran and shows a building under construction. *17th Century*

Ceramic bottle. *Reza Abbasi Muesum, Safavid Era*

Ladle and sweetmeat dish. *Freer Gallery of Art and Arthur Sackler Gallery, 12th & 14th century*

Did You Know?

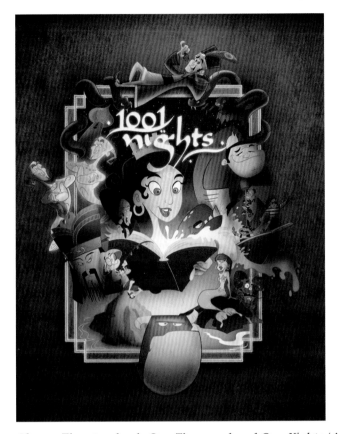

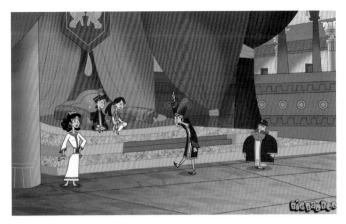

Above: The Barmakid were an aristocratic family from Iran and guardians of a Buddhist temple in Balkh (northern Afghanistan). The most famous Barmakid, Ja'far was the chief minister (grand vizier) to caliph Harun al-Rashid (r. 763 – 809). The character Ja'far in Aladdin, one of the stories from the book *1001 Nights* is very likely based on Ja'far Barmakid. The above image is a scene from *1001 Nights* .

Above: The storybook *One Thousand and One Nights* (*Arabian Nights*) was one of the many books that were re-written in Arabic. The book retold ancient tales from the pre-Islamic Iranian storybook *One Thousand Legends* (*Hizar Afsan*) along with new stories from many nations. This picture is from an animated production of *1001 Nights* by the Big Bad Boo Company which was co-founded by Shabnam Rezaei in New York.

Facing page: Miniature, showing the Biblical story of Noah's Ark, which is also in the Qur'an. *Gulistan Palace, Safavid Era*

Right: Several ports existed in the Persian Gulf since ancient times. Hormuz was one such port. It fell to the Arabs in 650 – 651. By the 10th century the town of Hormuz was a major port with many commercial ships carrying millet, indigo, cumin, slaves and sugarcane all over the area. Bowl showing a ship with captives. *Reza Abbasi Museum, 11th century*

Timeline of Medieval Iranian History & Art

640 – 750

Iran becomes a province of the Umayyad and Abbasid Islamic empires. An Iranian slave assassinates Umar the 2nd Caliph in 645. Major rebellions continue. Islamic art emerges greatly influenced by Sasanian and Byzantine artistic elements from antiquity, a creative factor that especially affected metalwork, textiles, and the depiction of animal, vegetal, and figural motifs. Iranian traditions continue but are gradually influenced by artistic trends from Damascus, Baghdad, and Samarra. The Arabs promote the Arabic language and Islamic culture and by 690 Arabic becomes the standard language of much of the Muslim world. Iranians maintain the Persian language.

750 – 900

Iranian bureaucrats gain key positions in the Arab courts. The architecture of mosques is influenced by Iranian styles and many mosques are built in Iran by the Arab dynasties. The oldest surviving ones are in Damghan, Isfahan, and Siraf. After the rise of local dynasties in the ninth century a rich and diverse artistic expression that is distinctly Islamic and Iranian emerges. The Islamic objection to figurative representations means calligraphy develops as a dominant art form. Tahirids, a local dynasty from Iran, practically end the Arab domination of Iran in 821 and by 837 the Saffarids of Sistan emerge as the main power in eastern Iran. The emergence of pro-Iranian dynasties results in the survival of Iranian cultural practices and the Persian language.

900 – 1000

The Buyids (945 - 1055), from north-central Iran capture Baghdad. The Samanids (864 - 1000) become the first Iranians ruling independently of Arabs. Persian replaces Arabic at the court. The Samanids' capital, Nishapur, becomes the artistic center of Iran and pre-Islamic traditions are revived and integrated into Islamic concepts. A new advanced under-glaze technique in ceramic making develops in Nishapur. The congregational mosques of Nayin, Niriz and Isfahan are among the few surviving buildings from the Samanid era. Monumental tombs are built. Some of the greatest literary and scientific masters such as Ferdowsi, Biruni, Ghazali and Avicenna are from this era.

1000 – 1220

Ghaznavids (975 - 1040), the first dominant Turkic group in Iran, are defeated by the Turkic Seljuqs (1040 - 1157) from Central Asia who occupied Baghdad and ended Buyid and Samanid rule. Innovation in arts and architecture during the Seljuq period had a major impact on later artistic developments. Bronze or brass objects were inlaid with copper, silver, gold and decorated with "animated" calligraphy. New techniques were developed in ceramic making and pottery including a luster technique from Kashan. The arts of book design and architecture reached new heights. In mosque architectural style, the courtyard with four vaulted halls (*iwans*) on each side, an influence from the Sasanian era, became prevalent.

1221 – 1353

Mongol conquests devastate the region. The Ilkhanid Mongols rule Iran (1256 - 1353) and end the caliphate in Baghdad. Tabriz in northwestern Iran becomes the artistic and cultural center of Iran. Oriental trends influence the existing Iranian-Islamic art and create new artistic innovations, profoundly affecting Islamic art from Anatolia to India. The arts of the book and illustrations advance, and both secular and religious art flourish. Monumental buildings such as the Ilkhanid palace at the ancient site, Takht -i- Suleiman in Azerbaijan, are built in addition to many mosques and shrines in cities across Iran including Ardabil, Isfahan, Zanjan, Natanz, Tabriz, Varamin, and Yazd.

1400 – 1501

The nomadic Turkmen group, Qara Quyunlu (1406 – 1469) establishes control over most of Iran and Iraq. Tabriz is revived as the capital (1406). Jahanshah Qara Quyunlu (r. 1439 – 1467), supports architecture and the book arts. The buildings Darb-i-Imam in Isfahan and the Blue Mosque in Tabriz are from this period. In 1469 the Aq Quyunlu Turkmen (1469 – 1508) take charge. They establish significant trade with Venice and play a role internationally. The relationship with Venice introduces European art and culture to Iranians. The Nasriyya complex in Tabriz is built by Uzun Hasan Aq Quyunlu (r. 1453 – 78), the grandfather of the first Safavid ruler, Shah Ismail. The Turkmen also supported the production of illustrated manuscripts.

1501 – 1722

Ismail Safavid (r. 1501 – 24) unites Iran and makes Shi'ism the state religion. The Safavids become major patrons of arts and architecture and build many bridges, roads, inns, commercial, religious and royal buildings, and improve communication and expand trade with Europe. The art of miniature and portrait painting flourishes and royal workshops for textile and carpets are set up in many cities. Extensive relations with Europeans impact the arts, particularly painting. Innovations in ceramics and pottery produce exquisite ware. Luxurious silks with gold and silver threads, and stunning designs, are exported globally. The Afghan revolt ends the Safavid rule in 1722.

Shah Abbas I

Early Islamic. *National Museum of Iran*

1360 – 1400

Short lived dynasties rule different parts of Iran after the Ilkhanid collapse. Under the Jalayirids (1360 - 1404), a Mongol family ruling Iraq and northwestern Iran, art and architecture remains the same, but the art of book illustration gains prominence. Timur's conquest of Iran (1389 - 1501) makes Iran part of a vast empire with cultural and artistic exchanges. The best artists and craftsmen are moved to Samarkand and then Herat. Sufi masters are supported, shrines and mosques are built. Multiple minarets, colourful tiles and huge domes are characteristics of architecture from the period. The Timurid artistic traditions greatly influence art and architecture in the region.

1726 – 1794

Nadir, working for a young Safavid monarch, forces the Afghans out of Iran and forms the Afsharid Dynasty (1736 – 1796). He regains all territory lost to the Ottomans and the Russians and defeats the Indians. Iran remains unstable and its economic and artistic development is halted. Karim Khan Zand occupies Isfahan in 1750, ends war, creates stability and founds the Zand Dynasty (1750 – 1794). He builds extensively in Shiraz and his patronage of art and literature allows Safavid traditions to continue into the next era. Then the Zands are defeated by Agha Mohammad Khan from the Qajar tribe. Iran enters the modern era.

Glossary

Abbasid Caliphate (750 – 1258): The Abbasids defeated the Umayyads, with help from Iranians, and became the third Islamic caliphate. They built Baghdad, and then after the sack of the city by the Mongols, they moved to Egypt and survived there until 1519.

Achaemenid (550 – 330 BCE): An Iranian dynasty and founders of the Persian Empire, the first great empire in antiquity. The Persian Empire extended from India to Egypt.

Afshars: A Turkic tribe in Iran. One of their leaders, Nadir Shah, ruled Iran briefly.

Anahita: The ancient Iranian goddess. She is associated with water and fertility, and was a patron of women and warriors. Her name means the "Immaculate One". She was popularized by the Achaemenids, and remained an important deity with major temples until the conquest of Islam.

Anatolia: A geographic region in Western Asia covering most of the modern Turkey.

Armenia (Ancient Urartu): A region and ancient kingdom comprised of parts of Asia Minor (Turkey) and the Caucasus. Armenia was the first country to adopt Christianity in CE 301.

Assyrian Christians: An ethnic group found mainly in Iraq with some adherents in Iran, Turkey and Syria. They claim descent from Ancient Assyria, a major kingdom in Mesopotamia and the eastern Mediterranean. They adopted Christianity between the first to third centuries.

Azerbaijan: The ancient Iranian province of Atropatene. Currently it is a province in Iran and an independent republic in southern Russia. The division happened in the 19th century when Iranians lost large territories to Russia.

Bakhtiari: An Iranian nomadic group regarded as Lurs and related to the Kurds.

Baluchi: An Iranian group and a language. They live in Eastern Iran, Pakistan and Southern Afghanistan.

Buyid Dynasty (945 – 1055): A pro-Shi'a Iranian dynasty originating in northern Iran. They controlled most of the area now covered by modern Iran and Iraq in the 10th and 11th centuries.

Circassian: A term applied to people from Northwest Caucasus.

Elam: A region in southern Iran. The Elamites (2700 – 539 BCE) formed the first independent kingdom in ancient Iran and ended Mesopotamian domination of Iran.

Farsi Dari: Also known as Eastern Persian, it is currently applied to the Persian dialect spoken in Afghanistan.

Farsi (Persian): An Iranian language spoken in Iran, Afghanistan, Tajikistan, Uzbekistan and by some in Iraq, Bahrain and Oman. It is Indo-European in origin.

Fatimid Dynasty (909 – 1171): The ruling Ismaili Shi'a dynasty of Egypt. They claimed descent from Fatima, the Prophet's daughter.

Georgia, the Republic: Located in the Caucasus region between Eastern Europe and Western Asia. Ancient Georgians adopted Christianity in the 4th century. The country was at times under Iranian control.

Ghaznavid (975 – 1040): The first Turkic group that ruled Iran. They were originally slaves serving the Iranian Samanid Dynasty.

History of Tabari: Written in Arabic by the Iranian scholar Mohammad ibn Jarir Tabari (838 – 923), the book is the most important history of the Middle East in the early Islamic period.

Imam Reza: The 8th Shi'a imam (9th century) and the crown prince and heir to the Abbasid throne. His shrine in Mashhad is a main pilgrim site for the Shi'ites.

Ring, *National Museum of Iran, early Islamic*

Islam: A monotheistic Abrahamic religion with around one billion adherents worldwide. Most Muslims belong to one of two major denominations, the Sunni and the Shi'a. Islam is the predominant religion in the Middle East.

Ismaili: Shi'a Muslims of many different ethnic backgrounds who are followers of the Agha Khan, a descendant of the Prophet Mohammad. They are dispersed on every continent and contribute to their communities as progressive modern Muslims.

Ja'fari Twelver Imami: The official Shi'a sect in Iran. Nadir Shah adopted the name in the 17th century. Twelver or Imami Shi'a is the largest branch of Shi'a Islam.

Jalayirids (1336 – 1432): A Mongol dynasty which ruled over Iraq and western Iran after the breakup of the Mongol Ilkhanid in Iran.

Kalila & Dimna: Translated into Middle Persian in 570 by the Iranian Borzuya from the Indian book *Panchatantra*, this animal fable was translated into Arabic in 750 by Roozbeh Farsi. Translated into 50 languages, the book is one of the most popular animal fables in history.

Kirman: A city and an ancient province; in the Persian period the province was called Karmania. It is located in southeastern Iran.

Khorasan: A large territory in Iran currently divided into three provinces. The ancient province was much larger and included Afghanistan, Turkmenistan, Uzbekistan and Tajikistan.

Kufic: An ancient Arabic script, Kufic was used for writing the first surviving Qur'ans. The name is derived from the city of Kufa in modern Iraq.

Kurds: An Iranian group mainly living in Iran, Turkey, Iraq and parts of Russia. Their language is northwestern Iranian. The province of Kurdistan in Iran is named after them.

Lurs: An Iranian group, they live mainly in west and southwestern Iran in Luristan Province. They are related to the Kurds.

Madrassa: The first known *madrassa* (Islamic educational school), was founded by a wealthy woman in Morocco. The Iranian Minister Nizam al-Mulk, created a network of *madrassa* schools in the 11th century. The most famous was Nizamieh in Baghdad.

Medes: An ancient tribe and the first Iranian rulers (612 – 550 BCE) of Mesopotamia.

Mesopotamia: Known as the "Cradle of Civilization", the ancient territory of Mesopotamia covered modern Iraq and parts of Iran, Syria and Turkey.

Middle Persian (Pahlavi): Both a script and a language, it was the dominant script in Iran from 224 to 651 during the Sasanian era.

Mithra (Mihr): An ancient Indo-Iranian deity popular in Iran that later became a major cult in Rome.

Mongols: An ethnic group mainly from Mongolia. Their first major leader, Genghis Khan, created the largest empire in the world by defeating and terrorizing many nations from China to Europe. The empire lasted from 1206 to 1368. Ghazan Khan (r. 1295 – 1304) the Ilkhanid ruler of Iran, was the first Mongol ruler to adopt Islam.

Muzaffarids (1314 – 1393): A short lived ruling group of Arab origin that briefly controlled central Iran in the 14th century after the collapse of the Ilkhanid Dynasty.

Parthians: An Iranian group who ruled Iran from 247 BCE to CE 224. They stopped Roman advances, through centuries of wars, into the east.

Qajar Dynasty (1795 – 1925): Formed by nomadic groups of Turkic origin in Iran.

Qashqa'i: A large nomadic group of Turkic origin in Iran. Thousands still practice nomadic life styles.

Ring. *National Museum of Iran, 11th century*

Rubaiyat: A book of poetry composed by Omar Khayyam (1048 – 1131). Its translation by Edward Fitzgerald into English made it a sensational success in Europe in the late 19th century with many Khayyam clubs. The London club lists people like James Joyce and Sir Arthur Conan Doyle, the creator of Sherlock Holmes, amongst its members.

Sarbadaran: A short-lived independent Iranian state in Khorasan after the collapse of the Ilkhanid state in the early 14th century.

Shi'a (Shi'ites): The second largest denomination in Islam, and the largest Muslim group in Iran. They believe Ali, the prophet's cousin and son-in-law is the only rightful successor to Prophet Mohammad. Currently, about 10% of all Muslims are Shi'ites.

Silk Road: An extensive network of tracks and roads, which connected China to Europe beginning in 206 BCE when a lucrative Chinese silk trade existed. The network lasted until around 1400.

Sunni: The largest branch of Islam. Sunni followers accept all first four caliphs, including Ali, as legitimate. Currently, there are about 8 million Sunni in Iran and 900 million globally.

Sogdian: A language and the name of an ancient Iranian dynasty which ruled territories in eastern Iran as far as Uzbekistan and Tajikistan.

Tajikistan: A republic in Central Asia. The country is populated by the Persian speaking Tajiks and in the medieval period was a major center of Iranian culture and art.

Taj Mahal: A mausoleum in Agra India built by the Mongol emperor, Shah Jahan for his deceased Iranian wife Mumtaz Mahal (d. 1632). He employed many Iranian architects and craftsmen to build the palace. Their descendants are still responsible for maintaining the complex.

Uzbekistan: A modern country occupied by the Uzbeks in the 16th century, Uzbekistan is located in Central Asia. It was once part of the Persian Samanid and the Tamerlane Empires.

Umayyad (661 – 750): The second Islamic caliphate, the Umayyads, had a major empire. After the Abbasids defeated them, they moved to Spain and created the Islamic dynasty of Cordoba.

Zoroastrians: Followers of the ancient Iranian prophet, Zoroaster (Zarathustra). Zoroastrianism was the religion of Iran from the sixth century BCE. Currently there are about 200,000 Zoroastrians globally. Important religious notions such as the coming of a saviour and the Last Judgment were articulated by this religion.

Left: Detail of miniature showing a king.
Reza Abbasi Museum, 17th century

Index

Left: Fresco. Shah Tahmasb Banquet. *Chihil Sutun Palace*

Acknowledgements

The publisher would like to thank: The Iranian Cultural Heritage Organization for permitting the photographing of objects at various museums in Tehran: Mr. Kargar, former Director, The National Museum of Iran; Mrs. Motamedi, former Executive Assistant to Director, The National Museum of Iran; Mrs. Zohreh Rohfar, Head, Islamic Collection; Mr. Vakili, Mr. Shahab Shahiri, Mrs. Fatemeh Hatami, Mrs. Zahra Akbari, Mrs. Nasrin Zehtab, Mrs. Leila Mohamadian, Mrs. Shahin Atefi and Mrs. Souri Ayazi at the National Museum of Iran; Mrs. Ahmadi, Director, Reza Abbasi Museum Tehran; Mrs. Seghat al-Islam, Director Gulistan Palace Museum; Abgineh Museum in Tehran; Betsy Kohut, Rights and Reproductions, Freer Gallery of Art and Arthur Sackler Gallery, Washington DC; Dr. Elena Stolyarik, Collections Manager, The American Numismatic Society; Art Resource, New York, representing: the Metropolitan Museum of Art and the Pierpont Morgan Library, New York; The British Museum and Victoria and Albert Museum, London; and Staatliche Museum zu Berlin, Germany.

The publisher would also like to thank Joachim Waibel and Zohreh Waibel, Parviz Tanavoli, Babak Manavi, Masoud Harati, Davood Sadeghsa, Freydis Jane Welland, Bita Tabrizi, John Scott, Dr. Gholamhossein Motamedi, Elham Puriamehr, Sheereen Price, Shabnam Rezaei, Shahrzad Akhavan, S.A. Concepts Corp., and A. Soudavar for providing several photos from his private collection. Photos of objects in the museums in Iran are by Davood Sadeghsa, all other photos from Iran are by Masoud Harati.

Art Direction	Photo Credits	Cover Design
Maral Honarbin	Davood Sadeghsa	Maral Honarbin
Malinda Dodds	Masoud Harati	
	J.M. Waibel	

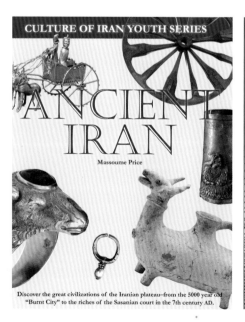

CULTURE OF IRAN YOUTH SERIES

ANCIENT IRAN

Massoume Price

Discover the great civilizations of the Iranian plateau–from the 5000 year old "Burnt City" to the riches of the Sasanian court in the 7th century AD.

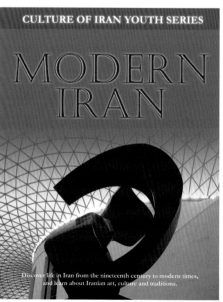

CULTURE OF IRAN YOUTH SERIES

MODERN IRAN

Discover life in Iran from the nineteenth century to modern times, and learn about Iranian art, culture and traditions.

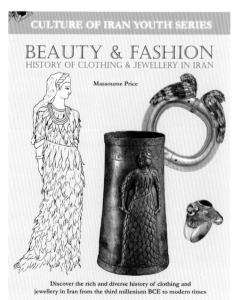

CULTURE OF IRAN YOUTH SERIES

BEAUTY & FASHION
HISTORY OF CLOTHING & JEWELLERY IN IRAN

Massoume Price

Discover the rich and diverse history of clothing and jewellery in Iran from the third millenium BCE to modern times